Please now accept this little gift,
An offering from the heart,
Its worth but small,
    its lines but few,
It breathes sincerest
    love for you.

With my love

O'er roses may
Your footsteps move,
Your smiles be
ever smiles of love

THE LOVEOMETER

The Thermometer of Love

M — Marriage.
A — Arrangements.
L — Love.
C — Courtship.
P — Partiality.
F — First Visit.

Thermometer of Love most pure
Show affection's temperature
Higher and still higher rise
Till I gain my wish'd for prize

A VICTORIAN BOOK OF LOVE

Forget Me Nots

By Cynthia Hart and
John Grossman
Text by Tracy Gill

WORKMAN PUBLISHING ♥ NEW YORK

For Harumi and Thomas,
with love. — C.H.

For my beloved Carolyn, and Jason and Jil. — J.G.

For Ardian and Jill, for endowing their children with a love
of words and beauty. — T.G.

For their generous loan of Victorian jewelry and objects for our photographs,
we thank Terry Rogers Vintage Jewelry, New York City; Nancy Marshall
Antique Collection, New York City; and Tail of the Yak, Berkeley, California.

For their gracious help and support, we thank Steven Tex, Petra Koencke,
John Freeman Gill, John Knuckey, Nancy Lindemeyer, Pat Clarkson, Irene
McGill, Pat Upton, The Ephemera Society of America and its president,
William F. Mobley, and everyone at Workman Publishing.

The photographic illustrations were created by Cynthia Hart and recorded on film by Steven Tex.
All the paper ephemera c. 1820–1920 is from the John Grossman Collection of Antique Images.

Library of Congress Cataloging-in-Publication Data
Hart, Cynthia. Forget-me-nots: a Victorian book of love / created by Cynthia Hart and John Grossman;
text by Tracy Gill.
p. cm. ISBN 0-89480-855-9
1. Courtship — Great Britain. 2. Courtship — United States. 3. Great Britain — Social life and customs — 19th
century. 4. United States — Social life and customs — 19th century. I. Grossman, John. II. Gill, Tracy. III. Title.
GT2743.H37 1990 392′.4′0941′ — dc20 90-50364 CIP

Workman Publishing
708 Broadway
New York, NY 10003
Printed in Japan
First printing September 1990
10 9 8 7 6 5 4 3 2 1

CONTENTS

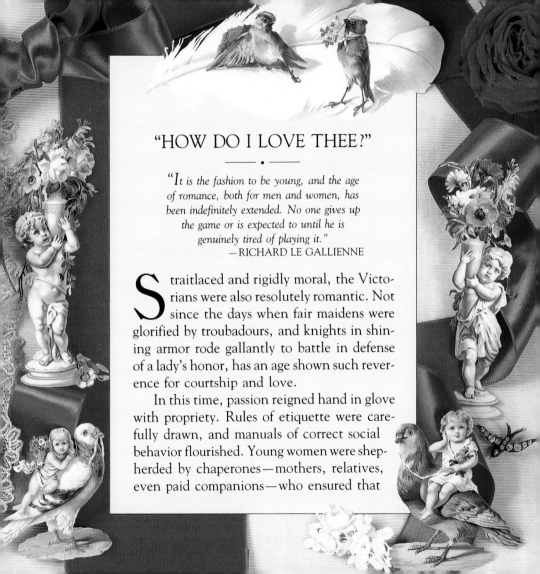

"HOW DO I LOVE THEE?"

— ⋅ —

"It is the fashion to be young, and the age of romance, both for men and women, has been indefinitely extended. No one gives up the game or is expected to until he is genuinely tired of playing it."
—RICHARD LE GALLIENNE

Straitlaced and rigidly moral, the Victorians were also resolutely romantic. Not since the days when fair maidens were glorified by troubadours, and knights in shining armor rode gallantly to battle in defense of a lady's honor, has an age shown such reverence for courtship and love.

In this time, passion reigned hand in glove with propriety. Rules of etiquette were carefully drawn, and manuals of correct social behavior flourished. Young women were shepherded by chaperones—mothers, relatives, even paid companions—who ensured that

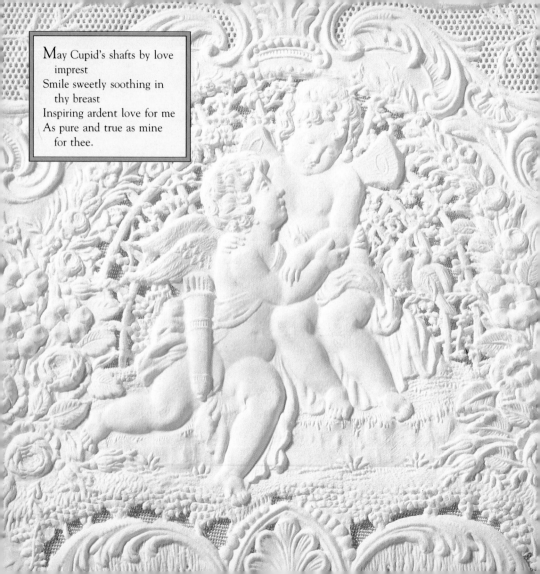

May Cupid's shafts by love
   imprest
Smile sweetly soothing in
   thy breast
Inspiring ardent love for me
As pure and true as mine
   for thee.

nothing *outré* or improper occurred. *Godey's Lady's Book* set the tone, publishing a mother's letter of "Advice to a Daughter" on appropriate deportment: "While you modestly accept any attentions which propriety warrants, let there be no attempt at artful insinuation on one hand, or taking a man's heart by storm on the other."

How, then, was an earnest suitor to know where he stood with his heart's desire? Always innovative, the Victorians simply invented new ways to play at the old game of courtship. Young ladies learned to signal their emotions with various items of apparel, and gentlemen quickly caught on to the subtleties of silent communication. Being handed a glove meant acceptance, whereas a mitten told a suitor to give up hope. Drawing a handkerchief across a cheek whispered "I love you"; twirling it in the right hand said sadly, "I love another."

"**All** things do go a-courting, in earth, or sea, or air, God hath made nothing single but thee in His world so fair!"
— *Emily Dickinson*

"**A**re we not
one? Are we not
joined by heaven?
Each interwoven
with the other's
fate?"

The Victorians were obsessively fond of
sport, and there were many public games that
fit very well with the private game of love.
Croquet, the popular pastime of the 1860s,
often allowed a daring glimpse of an ankle. In
the 1870s and '80s came "rinking," or roller
skating, and lawn tennis—pursuits that lifted
skirts even higher. Bicycling was soon to follow,
introducing a new mobility that permitted
couples to escape their chaperones—all in the
guise of health.

The strict code of proper moral conduct
also compelled the use of love tokens, whose
hidden meanings were recognizable only
to those versed in the language of romance.
Flowers were the most popular symbols,
and the most complex. Lovers had to be

familiar with a gardenful of meaning, including correct presentation, for a mistake could unintentionally spell the end of a relationship. (A flower handed stem first, for example, would convey a meaning exactly the opposite of what the flower stood for.)

When flowers seemed too temporal, the Victorian lover might send his betrothed a painted miniature, a brooch containing a woven lock of hair, or a piece of jewelry set with a gemstone of particular significance. The diamond, symbol of innocence, began its reign as *the* engagement stone. Some engaged men wore a "curb bracelet," which locked around the man's wrist and for which his fiancée kept the sole key.

No true romance could progress very far without some written affirmation of the heart. One woman, expressing her devotion in words that might not be spoken until after marriage, wrote to her future husband: "As well as I love my parents — as well as I love my connections to friends — Yet all *all* could I resign most willingly — most happily for *your* sake." Thus cards and love letters allowed unfettered expression of deep emotion. A first letter from a lover would be held most dear, and those that followed were increasingly so. This was true for both men and women, since letters were akin to personal visits. Of all the writings of the period, the intimate correspondence that survives today best depicts the Victorian ideal of love.

My heart goes bounding o'er the net, A "lose game" we begin, Before another sun has set I hope the game to win

St VALENTINE'S GREETINGS

My Valentine Greeting

My heart's a golf ball for your "game" you always with me "score." If I could only with "this" match you'd "tease" my heart no more.

You make ball of my heart, nd upon my soul, never be apart, hed the "Goal"!

THE CROQUET QUEEN

Her figure was faultless—nor tall, nor
   petite—
Her skirt barely touched the top lace of her
   boot;
I've seen in my time some remarkable feet,
But never one equalling that little foot.
Its *tournure* was perfect, from ankle to
   toe—
Praxiteles ne'er had such model for art—
No arrow so sharp ever shot Cupid's bow;
When poised on the ball it seemed to be
   pressing your heart!

"Love, faithful love, recalled thee to my mind—"
—William Wordsworth

In melody divine,
My heart it beats
to rapturous love,
I long to call
you mine.

"Forget me not where e'er you be, and I will ever think of thee."

To my Valentine

The violet loves a sunny
    bank,
The cowslip loves the
    lea;
The scarlet creeper loves
    the elm,
But I love,—thee! . . .

The Oriole weds his mottled
    mate,
The lily weds the bee;
Heaven's marriage ring is
    round the earth,
Let mine bind thee?

ALL THE WORLD
TO ME

— • —

Happy in our love to-day,
Light as air we sail away,
To my heart you hold the key,
For you're all the world to me.

TO MY LOVE

·

I doubt not thy loving
I doubt not thy word,
Still my heart is desponding to-day
If only one tone of thy sweet
    voice I heard—
Oh, send me a letter, I pray.

My heart doth beat
for thee alone.

Constant
and true.

Read in these flowers
And lines that I send
That the true love I bear thee
Death only can end!

Best
Wishes

There's none on earth ___ fair
As pure in thought ___ ___
To see thee is to love ___

If you will accept my heart,
You never will find one truer;
Then give me yours—so I remain
Your fond ___ ___ ___ wooer.

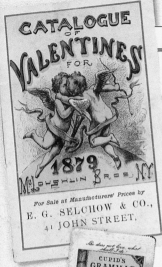

"CELEBRATIONS OF THE HEART"

— • —

*"I love thee to the level of every day's
Most quiet need, by sun and candlelight."*
— ELIZABETH BARRETT BROWNING

The Victorians loved to celebrate romance, and they never had long to wait before the calendar provided them with an appropriate occasion. Those who lived in the country, perhaps because of their daily exposure to natural beauty, were more likely to observe lustier love rituals. Yet even sophisticated urbanites, who might poke fun at the revels of their country cousins, took part in age-old rites of courtship and marriage.

Of all days of the year, none was more romantic than Valentine's Day — the undisputed favorite holiday of lovers the world over. From the simplest paper heart to tiered confections of gilded lace and powdered glass, valentines came into their own in the Victorian era. Lovers of a creative bent purchased Valentine Writers, little books containing verse for copying into "customized" cards: a woman denying a carpenter's hand because she found him "boring," or accepting a pastry chef because he was "sweet"; a gentleman addressing "a jealous lover" or "a lady that is fond of singing."

Throughout the spring, couples shared in the splendor of Nature's renewal. Though a religious

I think of thee at Eventide
When shines the star of Love —
When earth is garnished like a Bride,
And all is bright above —
I think of thee when orient day
Puts on its golden wings,
And mounts upon its bright'ning way,
  in beauty like the Spring.

holiday, Easter was the time for inscribing "paste" eggs with Cupids and lover's knots. May Day was an occasion for rejoicing, whether one fancied rising with the dawn to go "a-Maying" or dancing with jovial abandon around a beribboned maypole. June, "the month of marriages," was soon to follow; and for those who had not yet found the perfect partner, autumn and winter brought new opportunities for amorous pursuits.

Just as Nature's never-ending cycles were cause for celebra-

Waft of soul's
wing
What lies above?
Sunshine and
Love
Skyblue and
Spring!

—Robert
Browning

tion, so were birthdays, which cele-
brated the continuum of life. Queen
Victoria, with her own large family,
popularized birthday parties for chil-
dren, encouraging recognition of
each child's importance in the world.
Other anniversaries, such as wed-
dings, were similarly noted. A matron
could expect to receive mementos
acknowledging the number of years
she had been married or honoring

her for the children she had produced. Among popular tokens were brooches set with gemstones of particular significance (a garnet or topaz for unwavering devotion, moonstones to arouse tender passions) or "Regard" rings, which used the first initial of each set stone to spell a single word of endearment. Husband and wife might share a private anniversary of the day they met, or a memory of their first kiss, or the day he finally proposed.

The faithful Victorians emphasized the importance of constancy, even if only to a memory. For, however profuse their memories of happy occasions, reminders of bitter-sweet moments were common. A love unrequited, a love won and lost, or a single, never-to-be-repeated embrace lived on in a lover's heart. Just as a love letter might have been kissed upon its first receipt, a packet of such epistles, tied with a blue satin ribbon, would be kissed again— on particular days when memory gave a noticeable tug on one's heartstrings.

I can boast nor wealth nor birth
Think you these alone have worth
Surely health a heart that's true
A hand that can protect you too,
Are gems, and these I proffer you.

Thou art all the world
    To this heart of mine;
Life, and its tender hopes
    Are thine—and only thine.
Ah! love, wilt thou to me,
    Be more than Valentine?

A MATCH

If love were what the rose is,
  And I were like the leaf,
Our lives would grow together
In sad or singing weather,
Blown fields or flowerful closes,
  Green pleasure or grey grief;
If love were what the rose is,
  And I were like the leaf.

If I were what the words are,
  And love were like the tune,
With double sound and single
Delight our lips would mingle,
With kisses glad as birds are
  That get sweet rain at noon;
If I were what the words are,
  And love were like the tune . . .

If you were April's lady,
  And I were lord in May,
We'd throw with leaves for hours
And draw for days with flowers,
Till day like night were shady
  And night were bright like day;
If you were April's lady,
  And I were lord in May.

—Algernon Charles Swinburne

Where *can* the postman be, I say?
He ought to *fly*—on such a day!
Of *all* days in the year, you know,
It's monstrous rude to be so *slow*:
The fellow's so *exceeding* stupid—
Hark!—*there* he is! oh! the *dear* CUPID!

To my Valentine.

Thou art my joy,
my life, my light,
And all my hopes are thine,
So trust me near,
and out of sight,
My fond, fair
Valentine.

Let me dwell in the light of thine eyes,
    Let me find a sweet home in thy heart!
For my soul like a wild bird flies,
    To linger wherever thou art —
        As night gives place to the day,
            And darkness before the sun flies,
So my sorrows will all melt away,
            When I live in the light
                of thine eyes.

To My sweet Valentine

Sweet one for whom I long have sighed,
O cast one loving glance
on me!
Though all the world should frown beside,
Thy love alone my crown
should be;
And my devoted, grateful heart
Should turn in rapture
unto thee,
If thou wouldst bend those gentle eyes
With tender love and trust
on me.
Could such a fate as this be mine,
'Twould be a glimpse of
love divine,
And never should I seek to gain
Release from love's delicious
chain.

"I THEE WED"

"Come, let's be a comfortable couple and take care of each other! How glad we shall be, that we have somebody we are fond of always, to talk to and sit with. Let's be a comfortable couple. Now do, my dear!"
—*CHARLES DICKENS*

Only marriage and children could fill a house with the true love that Victorians so revered. And in matters of the heart, the best role model conceivable was the Queen herself—a wife and mother who put love for her family above many affairs of state.

From the outset, bridal couples followed

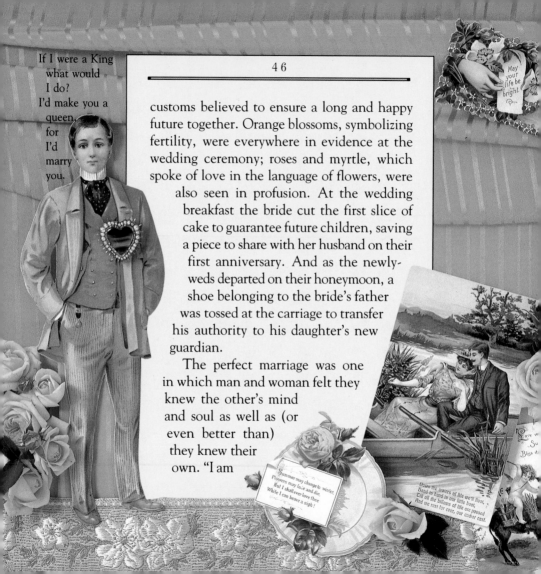

If I were a King
what would
I do?
I'd make you a
queen,
for
I'd
marry
you.

customs believed to ensure a long and happy future together. Orange blossoms, symbolizing fertility, were everywhere in evidence at the wedding ceremony; roses and myrtle, which spoke of love in the language of flowers, were also seen in profusion. At the wedding breakfast the bride cut the first slice of cake to guarantee future children, saving a piece to share with her husband on their first anniversary. And as the newly-weds departed on their honeymoon, a shoe belonging to the bride's father was tossed at the carriage to transfer his authority to his daughter's new guardian.

The perfect marriage was one in which man and woman felt they knew the other's mind and soul as well as (or even better than) they knew their own. "I am

May your life be bright.

Summer may change to winter,
Flowers may fade and die,
But I shall ever love thee
While I can heave a sigh!

familiar with your inner heart, as with my home," Nathaniel Hawthorne wrote to his Sophia, "but yet there is a sense of revelation—or perhaps a recovered intimacy with a dearest friend long hidden from me."

Victorian men and women greatly appreciated those very qualities that made them so wonderfully distinct from one another. In the nineteenth century, a man was a man, preferably a gentleman, and a woman was undeniably a lady, uniquely feminine. Though their separate domains sometimes overlapped, competition within the marriage was unheard of. Man might publicly jest about his wife's control over the home, but he nonetheless loved her for managing his domestic life better

THE WISH

I've often wished to have a friend
With whom my choicest hours to
   spend,
To whom I safely may impart
Each wish and weakness of my
   heart.
Who would in every sorrow
   cheer,
And mingle with my grief a tear,
And to secure that bliss for life,
I'd like that friend to be my wife.

A feast of flowers here behold
   A thing of joy to see
But ah! to me 'tis sweeter far
   To feast mine eyes on thee!

LOVE RETURNED

— • —

How sweet the love
   that meets return,
How dear the sunny smile,
Lighting up eyes
   that on us burn
With love lights
   all the while.
How soft the sigh
   breathed forth by lips
That speak love's tender vow,
Cheering the heart
   as sunlight tips
The hills with golden glow.

— • —

Married.
At North Bennington, Vt., August 30th 1871.
John G. McCullough,
to
Lizzie Hall Park,
Daughter of T. W. & Laura V. H. Park.

than he ever could alone. Many Victorians considered that the more accomplished each partner in his or her own right, the stronger the union (as long as each partner respected his or her God-given role).

Marriage was the safe haven for two beloved souls, and children were the purest symbol of the romantic bond that united them. As constant reminders of the true love shared by

I am yours
forever
And our co-equal
love
will make the
stars
to laugh with
joy . . .

—Christina
Walsh

Marriage Reception
OF
Barkis and Pe...

Souvenir.

Papa and Mama, sons and daughters were held most dear to the Victorian heart. Petted and coddled, badgered and disciplined, they were taught early on that their reason for existence was to eventually be responsible and loving adults. Parents had a duty to their children to rear them wisely and to teach them propriety, a duty that could only be accomplished with understanding and love.

In a society where family was prized above all else, those denied matrimonial bliss were ofttimes looked at askance. By the ripe old age of twenty-five, a woman would begin to hear whispers of her imminent spinsterhood; by thirty, she was considered beyond picking. A gentleman might maintain his bachelorhood with a jaunty air until the age of forty, when he was considered a confirmed bachelor and often permitted a certain crusty edge to his demeanor. (The ubiquitous etiquette books, of course, printed long lists

of "Don'ts" for the unmarried man, encouraging polite behavior and unrumpled clothing.) Society sometimes regarded the bachelor with dismay, for he might have made a personal choice to remain single—thus willfully neglecting his duty to future generations. Only if he lamented a lost love and an irreparably broken heart would he be entirely forgiven, for the Victorians believed that true love would come to anyone who looked for it in the proper manner.

True love was a priceless treasure, not willingly parted with for even a moment. In diaries and love letters, married men and women lamented even the briefest of separations, finding life without the other virtually unbearable. "Can I—Oh! can I, wait so long?" was the burning query sent to Mabel Loomis

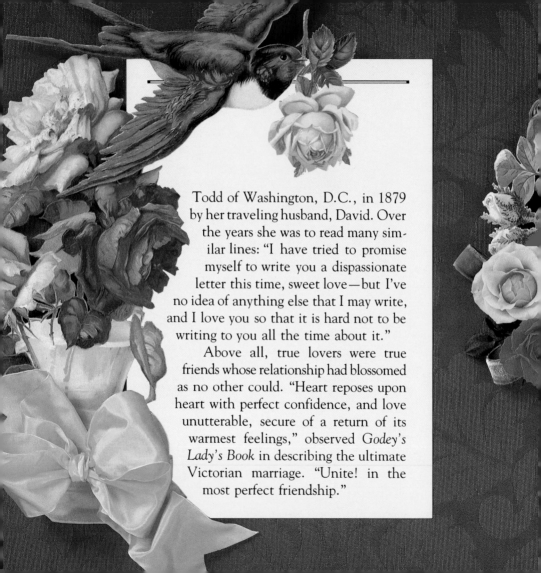

Todd of Washington, D.C., in 1879 by her traveling husband, David. Over the years she was to read many similar lines: "I have tried to promise myself to write you a dispassionate letter this time, sweet love—but I've no idea of anything else that I may write, and I love you so that it is hard not to be writing to you all the time about it."

Above all, true lovers were true friends whose relationship had blossomed as no other could. "Heart reposes upon heart with perfect confidence, and love unutterable, secure of a return of its warmest feelings," observed *Godey's Lady's Book* in describing the ultimate Victorian marriage. "Unite! in the most perfect friendship."

"May loving angels guard and keep thee, ever pure as thou art now."

To my
Valentine.

Pray think of me when flowers you view:
Their beauties all expressed in you.

Pray think of m...
With you I coul...

A DAISY CHAIN

Go, sweet token, with my love,
    To my Valentine,
Say that love doth hold in chains,
    All this heart of mine . . .
Take my greeting, then, and say
    I shall happy be,
If in sweet return for mine,
    My true love loves me.

are sad:
glad.

And when you wander far and wide,
    How fain I'd wander by your side.

"FORGET NOT THY FRIEND"

— • —

*"Do you know what friendship is?
—Yes—it is to be as brother and sister, two souls
which touch each other without meeting, like two
fingers on the same hand."*
—GODEY'S LADY'S BOOK

From earliest childhood, Victorians learned the value of friendship. Hand in hand, young girls ventured forth to gather wildflowers to press and make into gift cards; together they learned how to decorate the home and cook nourishing meals. They pored over ladies' magazines and studied their older sisters' wardrobes, all the while forming strong bonds that would last them through courtship, marriage and the rearing of their own large broods. Girlfriends were often called "sister," implying a heartfelt intimacy.

DEVOTION

— • —

On the Shore—or on the Sea—
Thou, art all in all to me.
Yes! in love's divine emotion,
Read—oh! read—my Soul's devotion.

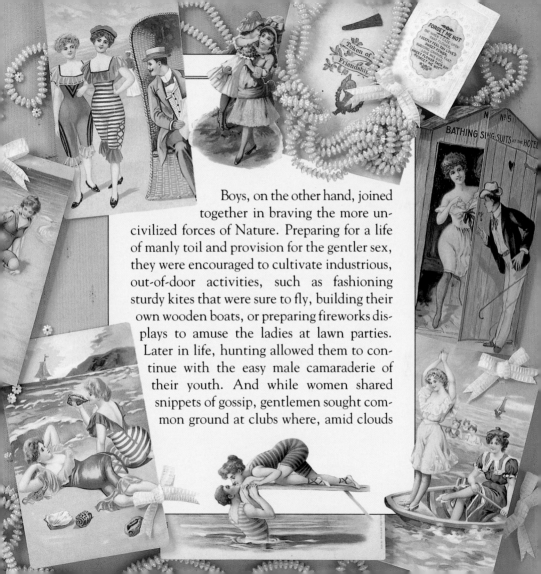

Boys, on the other hand, joined together in braving the more uncivilized forces of Nature. Preparing for a life of manly toil and provision for the gentler sex, they were encouraged to cultivate industrious, out-of-door activities, such as fashioning sturdy kites that were sure to fly, building their own wooden boats, or preparing fireworks displays to amuse the ladies at lawn parties. Later in life, hunting allowed them to continue with the easy male camaraderie of their youth. And while women shared snippets of gossip, gentlemen sought common ground at clubs where, amid clouds of pungent cigar smoke (which any well-bred lady would cringe to have in her home parlor), they told tall tales, spoke of sweethearts with discreet ardor, and helped compatriots establish proper social connections.

In keeping with the Victorian passion for mementos, friendship jewelry was regularly exchanged. Popular symbols that bespoke the giver's heart included the anchor of hope and the single Hebrew word *Mizpah*, which meant "The Lord watch between thee and me when we are absent from one another." The latter, inscribed on bracelets, brooches and rings, was an appropriate sentiment for women to share with women and for men to share with men. Sir J.M. Barrie, author of *Peter Pan*, fondly recalled in 1896 that his mother, after receiving a *Mizpah* ring, "did carry that finger in such a way that the most reluctant must see."

Other very popular friendship tokens were made of coins, fashioned either at

With love and best wishes.

While the bright sun doth shine I'll ne'er forget thee.

home or by a jeweler. Silver coins were smoothed on one side, engraved with fancy designs, initials and commemorative messages, and worn as pins, pendants or charms. Beginning in 1884 and gaining popularity with Victoria's Jubilee coinage in 1887, enameled tokens were made by cutting into existing coins, then baking on painted designs.

Friendship quilts were also the rage in America at this time. These were made of squares of fabric, often from friends' dresses, with signatures in ink or stitched carefully right onto the cloth. Loving poems and pleas to remember a friend's smiling face always, no matter how far from home the quilt's owner might wander in this new age of expansion, filled all availa-

ble white space on the fabric. Today, their sweet inscriptions remind us of the dilemma of nineteenth-century society, as industrialization and new careers forced friends apart: "Tho' far away from thee I roam,/ Forget thee I can never;/For all the joy this life affords/Is centered in thee ever."

Similarly, little autograph books were kept by women and children (and sometimes men, too), who would ask friends and relatives to scribble a few affectionate lines. Usually the signer would write a verse wishing the book's owner future luck in love or life. Sometimes the wish was simply to be remembered. And sometimes elaborate tokens were

pasted onto the album's pages: plaited hair, pressed flowers, colored ribbons and die-cut scrap, elaborate calligraphy and personalized watercolor or pen-and-ink drawings of familiar scenes.

Next to the diary, lovingly filled with private thoughts and events, the autograph album was perhaps the most personal record of the history of its owner and her friends. Births, graduations, changes of residence and even deaths were noted and sometimes marked with a small and lasting token of remembrance.

"This album is a garden spot, where all your friends may sow," Nellie S. King of Perry, Iowa, would write to her friend Mrs. Filkins in September 1884. "I'll plant the seeds forget-me-not, and hope that they may grow."

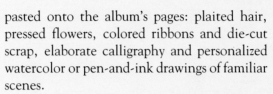

Loyal friendship
Pure and true,
Such is what
I feel for you.

MY OWN SWEET VALENTINE

—— · ——

Like the sweetly
  budding rose,
Freshened by the
  gentle rain;
Like the Evening Star
  that glows,
Brightest of
  the starry train;

Like a well
  arranged BOUQUET,
Where the fairest
  flowers combine,
Odours rich
  and colours gay,
Is my own
  sweet Valentine.

"*Fresh as the flowers may all your pleasures be.*"

With thoughts of thee my heart is laden

PANSY

THINK OF ME

Pray you, love, remember
There is Pansies . thats for thoughts

Shakespeare.

ENT. STA. HALL.

Yours
for ever.

SINCERE FRIENDSHIP

— • —

Friendship! now I love
   the feeling,
Sweetly soothing
   to the mind,
When o'er my soul
   sweet mem'ry stealing,
Leaves a holy
   calm behind.
Then to Fancy's
   eye appearing,
Forms beloved,
   tho' distant far,
Wake affection's
   glowing feeling,
Silence every
   passion's jar.

To my Valentine!

Here is a little forest,
Whose leaf is ever green;
Here is a brighter garden,
Where not a frost has been;
In its unfading flowers
I hear the bright bee hum;
Prithee, my brother,
Into *my* garden come!

—Emily Dickinson

LOVE'S CABLE.

"Forget me not!
No other heart
Can ever be more
true than mine.
Though many loving
friends surround
Thy sunny path,
my Valentine."

Unless otherwise noted, all antique paper ephemera items reproduced in this book were originally printed by the nineteenth-century color process of chromolithography. Descriptions of items read clockwise, beginning at the center top of each page.

Selections of period valentine verse appear throughout the book and are identified in these pages only in noting relevant detail.

Endsheets: Valentine paper lace; die cut, embossed; c1880. Scrap; die cut, embossed; c1880. **P.5:** Valentine sachet; embossed paper lace, gathered silk netting bound with silver wire, applied scrap; c1880. **P.6:** Valentine; 9¼"h × 8"w; paper lace, gilded, theorem work, applied scrap, silk netting, embossed silver foil applied from behind; c1870. Valentine sachet; paper lace envelope, embossed, gilded, scrap border mounted on paper springs; c1875. Cloth label; silver foil over paper, die cut, embossed, gummed; c1875. **P.7:** Valentine; paper lace, hand-colored, silk ribbon bow, applied printed, hand-cut thermometer (pull tab causes silver foil "mercury" column to rise or fall); English; c1860. Valentine; silvered paper lace, applied scrap, dyed feathers, cloth flowers, pearls, green glass jewels, silk netting, gilded springwire; c1875. Valentine; die cut, embossed, silver, applied scrap; c1880. **P.8:** Lace handkerchief; c1890. Baroque pearls; c1880, courtesy Kathy Riedesel. Scrap; die cut, embossed; c1895. Visiting card (scrap lifts to reveal hidden name); c1880. **P.9:** Cherubs; stamped brass; c1980. Scrap; die cut, embossed; c1885. **P.10:** Valentine cameo paper lace blank; die cut, embossed; c1875. Valentine; cameo paper lace, Meek, die cut, embossed; Whitney, maker; c1880. **P.11:** Valentine; cameo paper lace (lifts to reveal pink paper with applied chromolithograph and greeting); Kershaw, die cut, embossed; Whitney, maker; c1880. Valentine (face); cameo paper lace, die cut, embossed; applied scrap, paper wafers;

c1875. Valentine (face); cameo paper lace, die cut, embossed; c1875. Buttons; cloisonné enamel and hand-painted; c1880–90. **P.12** Daisy table scarf; silk, lace; c1880. Floral spray pin; carved ivory; c1880. Bird pin; paste, silver; c1900. Bird pin; diamonds, pearl, ruby, silver; c1890. Scrap; die cut, embossed; c1890.

"HOW DO I LOVE THEE?"

P.13: Epigraph from *Vanishing Roads*. Bird pin; paste, silver; c1900. Floral spray pin; carved ivory; c1880. Scrap; die cut, embossed; c1890. **P.14:** Cameo paper lace (enlargement); detail of valentine, watermarked Towgood; 1852. **P.15:** Paper lace; detail of valentine; Mansell; inscribed 1852. Lover's greeting card, "Freundschaftskarten"; embossed gold foil border, mesh, hand-painted and assembled; Johann Endletzbergen, Vienna; c1820. **P.16:** "Are we not one . . ." Handwritten verse on valentine sent in 1852 to Miss Maria L. Greene, N.Y.C. Valentine; embossed border, mezzotint engraving, hand-colored; English, c1850. Lover's-knot valentine; letterpress, hand-ruled borders on thin paper; c1850. Valentines; embossed border, mezzotint engraving, hand-colored; English; c1850. **P.17:** Valentines; Rebus; hand-colored, die-cut edge; c1860. Embossed border, mezzotint engraving, hand-colored; English;

c1850. Advertising handout; embossed, letterpress copy; E.E. King; London; c1870. **P.18:** Dress appliqué, glass beads, faux pearls; c1910. Postcard; embossed, gilded; John Winsch; 1911. Trade card; die cut, easel back; A.G. Spalding; Koerner & Hayes, lithographers; Buffalo, N.Y.; c1895. Postcards: H. Latzkaa, artist; Germany; c1910. Embossed, gilded; John Winsch; 1911. Album scrap; c1880. **P.19:** Postcards: Embossed, gilded; John Winsch; 1910, 1911. Belgium; postmarked 1909. Album scrap; c1880. Grape pin; glass, brass; c1900. Ribbon flower; silk, velvet; c1920. **P.20:** Scrap; die cut, embossed; c1885. Cupid buttons; hand-painted; c 1870. Buttons; cloisonné enamel and hand-painted, cut steel; c1880. Paper lace doily; c1900. Miniature motto cards; c1885. **P.21:** Scrap; die cut, embossed; c1885. Applied silk clothing; Germany; c1890. **P.22:** Foldout valentine; 9⅝"h × 8¼"w; 3' stages, die cut, embossed, gilded, applied scrap; c1910. Ostrich feather fan; c1890. Quill; hand-painted, bronze holder and pen nib; c1875. Foldout valentine; 4 stages, die cut, embossed, applied scrap, honeycomb tissue; c1910. Mechanical friendship card (silk ribbon pull tab reveals celebration scene); die cut, embossed, gilded border, applied scrap; c1880. **P.23:** Valentine; die cut, embossed, gathered blue silk, embossed, gilded oval, woven silk center; c1885. Quill; hand-painted, bronze holder and pen nib; c1875. Pull-down valentine; 3 stages, die cut, embossed, applied scrap, honeycomb tissue; inscribed 1904. Letter seals: Hand-painted china and brass; c1900. Gold and agate; c1880. Mechanical friendship card (pull tab extends petals); die cut, embossed, gilded border, applied scrap; c1880. **P.24:** "Happy in our love . . ." from an Ernest Niser (London) valentine signed "H.G.H." Foldout valentine (hidden strings form boat shape); 9¼ × 12"w; 4 stages, die cut, embossed, gilded, applied scrap, honeycomb tissue, printed tis-

To my Valentine

sue; c1915. **P.25:** Foldout valentine (hidden strings form boat shape); 10⅛"h × 12¼"h; 3 stages, die cut, embossed, applied scrap, honeycomb tissue; c1915. Valentine; die cut, embossed, gilded; c1880. **P.26:** Hidden-name visiting card (applied scrap lifts to reveal name); c1885. Valentine; c1880. Pen; mother-of-pearl, gold; c1870. Lady's envelope; motto paper wafer on flap; 1853. Letter to friend; Kennebunk, Me.; August 24, 1853. Lady's envelope; embossed initial "B"; postmarked Kansasville, Wisc.; c1868. Friendship cards; die cut, embossed; c1885. **P.27:** Foldout valentine (table forms, flowers stand up); c1905. Calling-card case; mother-of-pearl mosaic; c1880. **P.28:** Valentine "beehive" (enlargement, original 2¾" diameter); shown raised, revealing hand-colored lithograph; printed, die cut tissue, silk tassel, bronze ink, embossed border; c1860.

"CELEBRATIONS OF THE HEART"

P.29: Valentine verse booklets (preprinted verses to cut out and paste into valentines): 16 pp., McLoughlin, N.Y., 1880; 34 pp., T.W. Strong, N.Y. 1860; 32 pp., C.P. Huestis, N.Y. (Geo. Snyder, lithographer, N.Y.), 1846. Valentine; "beehive" (see p. 38). Valentine (book opens to reveal illustration); die cut, embossed border; c1865. Valentine catalog; 16 pp.; McLoughlin, N.Y.; 1879. **P.30:** Glue pot; crystal, silver; c1890. Scrap uncut sheet; die cut, embossed; c1885. Scraps: die cut, embossed; c1885. Pen; carved bone, brass; c1880. Scissors; silver; c1890. Valentine lace; die cut, embossed, gilded; c1880. Preprinted valentine verses; c1880. Scrap: die cut, embossed; c1885. Miniature box in form of book; embossed gold foil over cardboard; c1880. Album picture; c1880. Scrap uncut sheet; die cut, embossed; c1885. **P.31:** Valentine; 11"h × 8"w; 3 layers, embossed silvered border, gilded paper lace, applied scrap, silk ribbon, paper springs;

c1895. Scrap uncut sheet; die cut, embossed; c1885. Valentine papers; c1885. Dresden ornament (candy container); embossed glazed paper over cardboard, embossed gold trim, applied scrap; c1890. Scrap uncut sheet; die cut, embossed; c1885. Dresden stars, trim; gold foil over embossed paper; c1900. Dresden ornament (candy container); embossed foil over cardboard; c1890. Album picture; c1885. Scrap; die cut, embossed; c1885. Valentine papers; embossed; c1880. **P.32:** Hidden-message friendship card, (various layers lift to reveal messages); 3 layers, die cut, embossed, gilded border, applied scrap; c1880. Foldout valentine (wheels turn); 4 layers, die cut, embossed; Germany; c1910. Friendship card, (center oval drops down, lifting 2 layers to reveal hidden illustration); 4 layers, die cut, embossed, gilded borders, applied scrap; c1880. Mechanical friendship card (pull tab lifts flap to extend hidden scene); 3 stages, die cut, embossed, gilded border, applied scrap; c1880. **P.33:** Mechanical friendship card (silk ribbon pull tab drops flowers to reveal hidden messages and pictures); die cut, embossed, gilded border, applied scrap layers; c1880. Foldout valentine; 4 layers, die cut, embossed, applied scrap, honeycomb tissue; c1895. Mechanical friendship card; (pull tab activates scene); 4 layers, die cut, embossed, applied scrap; Germany; c1890. Scrap; die cut, embossed; c1885. Mechanical friendship card (silk ribbon pull tab raises child's arm

revealing message); die cut, embossed border, applied scrap; c1880. **P.34:** Cameos; carved shell, gold filigree; c1910. **P.35:** Drop valentine panel; die cut, Raphael Tuck, London; printed in Saxony; c1900. **P.36:** Scrap; die cut, embossed; Friedberg & Silberstein, Germany; c1880. Boxed valentine; four layers, paper lace, gilded paper lace, die cut, embossed, applied scrap, silk netting center, silk ribbon, cloth flowers, gold stars; c1875. Drop valentine figure (placed on boxed valentine); die cut, embossed, gilded; Ernest Nister; c1895. Postcard; die cut, embossed; Germany; postmarked 1909. **P.37:** Scarf; silk chiffon; c1915. Mechanical valentine; 8¼"h × 6"w; die cut, embossed, gilded, applied scrap figures; c1910. Scrap; die cut, embossed; 1890. **P.38:** "Where can the postman be . . . " from *Hone's Every-Day Book* (1826). Necklaces; Venetian glass beads; c1900. Scrap; die cut, embossed; c1890. Shaped trade card (Foster's Kid Gloves); 1890. Dance program, opened (flower scrap hinged on silk ribbons drop to reveal hidden messages, pictures); die cut, embossed, gilded, silvered paper lace, applied scrap, silk cord, tassel; 1874. Foldout valentine; die cut, embossed; c1910. Love token (opens to reveal hidden message); die cut, embossed, applied scrap; c1870. **P.39:** Buttons; glass paperweight; c1900. Foldout valentine; 9½"h × 9⅜"w; 3 layers, die cut, embossed, gilded, applied scrap; c1910. Baptismal commemorative; embossed, gilded envelope; applied gathered netting, silk ribbon, silvered paper lace, gold stars, blue foil, gold cherub ornament; baptismal certificate inside; Germany; c1890. Dresden ornament (candy container); silk over cardboard, embossed gold foil trim, silk ribbon, gold foil ornament; Germany 1890. **P.40:** Foldout valentine; 10⅛"h × 10"w; 3 layers, die cut, embossed, gold stamped greeting; c1905. Flower spray pin; garnets, brass; c1880. **P.41:** Stock calendar illustration; die cut, embossed, gilded, center space for imprint and calendar pad;

c1910. Bows, cutwork appliqués, metallic threads; c1900. Oval pin; garnet, gold; c1880. **P.42:** Hanging valentine; 6"h x 6¼"w; die cut, embossed, gold-stamped greeting, foldback wings, gold cord; c1905. **P.43:** Filigree comb; gold onlay, tortoiseshell; c1880. Ladies' pocket watch; gold; c1890. Jewel box; brass, fabric-lined; c1880. Heart charms, bracelet; gold wash; c1890. Match safe; gold; c1890. Lorgnette; gold; c1895. **P.44:** Children's book cover (*Two Little Playmates*); 13¼"h × 10"w; Frances Brundage, artist; M.A. Donohue; 1913.

"I THEE WED"

P.45: Foldout valentines: 2 stages, die cut, embossed, c1910; 2 stages, die cut, embossed, honeycomb tissue heart, silk ribbon, c1910. **P.46:** Friendship card; die cut, embossed; c1895. Postcard; embossed, Paul Finkenrath; Berlin; postmarked 1913. Love token; die cut, embossed; c1885. Paper doll; 9¼"h; easel back; artistic series no. 601; Raphael Tuck, London; 1894. Heart pin; agate, pearl; c1820. **P.47:** Paper doll; 10¼"h; easel back; artistic series no. 601; Raphael Tuck, London; 1894. Love token; die cut, embossed; c1885. Postcards: Embossed, International Art Publ. Co., N.Y.; printed in Germany; postmarked 1909. Embossed; Paul Finkenrath, Berlin; c1910. Hand pin; resin, paste, gold; c1880. Heart locket; Mexican; gold, coral beads; c1960. **P.48:** Box label; 15"h x 11"w; embossed, gilded, printed one color, hand-painted accents; c1870. Friendship card; die cut, embossed, gilded; c1860. Stock trade card; jeweler imprint, embossed, gilded; Geo. Brunswick, lithographer, N.Y.; 1903. Box label; die cut, embossed, gilded; chromolithograph applied from behind; c1870. Scrap; die cut, embossed; c1885. Cloth label; embossed, gilded, applied Baxter print; c1860. Friendship card; embossed, gilded, c1870. Valentine; die cut, embossed,

gilded; Ernest Nister, London; printed in Bavaria; c1895. Buttons; brass, glass, mother-of-pearl; c1880–1900. Moss Rose pin; silver and gold wash; c1870. **P.49** Cloth label; die cut, embossed, gilded; c1860. Lover's greeting card ("Freundschaftskarten"); embossed, mesh center, applied gold foil embossed ornaments and trim, hand-painted scrap; Anton Peter, Vienna; c1820. Box label; 11⅞"h × 8⅝"w; embossed, gilded, printed one color, hand-painted accents; c1870. Baptismal commemorative envelope; embossed, gilded, applied mesh, silver and gold foil ornaments, scrap, silver foil; c1870. Oval box label; embossed, gilded, chromolithograph applied from behind; c1870. Box label; die cut, embossed, gilded; chromolithograph applied from behind; c1870. Charm string; c1990, created from buttons c1870–1900; courtesy Caroline Shearer. **P.50:** Mock orange blossoms; wax and fabric, c1900. Wedding ring; pearls, garnet, gold; c1880. Marriage reception invitation; c1875. Pin and framed oval drop; hand-painted miniature on ivory, natural pearls, gold; c1880. Birds-on-fence pin; rose-cut diamonds, silver set, gold back; c1850. Scrap; die cut, embossed; c1885. Marriage announcement; engraved; 1871. **P.51:** Necklace; gold, natural pearls; c1890. Paper doll; 9"h; "Bell of Saratoga"; Marguerite McDonald, artist; Raphael Tuck, London; 1894. Valentine (pull tab raises center panel to reveal message); embossed, gilded border,

applied scrap, hand-painted; c1845. Box; enamel with gold inlay and trim; c1890. Crescent pin; natural pearls, brass; c1890. Scrap; die cut, embossed; c1885. Wedding souvenir card; die cut, embossed, applied silk; silver foil behind man's ring; c1895. Valentine; cameo lace, Berlin & Jones, applied scrap, paper wafers; Whitney; c1875. **P.52:** Scrap; die cut, embossed; c1885. Valentine; gilded paper lace, hand-painted, printed silk center; c1865. Postcard; c1900. Advertising calendar; Scott's Emulsion; 1894. Scrap; die cut, embossed; c1880. Postcard; embossed; Germany; c1910. Valentine; die cut, embossed, applied scrap, printed silk center; c1860. Scrap; die cut, embossed; c1880. Postcard; c1900. **P.53:** Postcard; Paul Finkenrath, Berlin; c1910. Scrap; die cut, embossed; c1885. Sachets: Paper lace border, gilded; c1865. Paper lace, chromolithograph applied from behind; c1870. Shaped trade card; Peek, Frean's Biscuits; c1895. Valentine; cameo paper lace, Wood, printed silk applied from behind; c1865. Scrap; die cut, embossed; c1885. Postcard; c1905. Scrap; die cut, embossed; c1890. Shaped valentine; die cut, embossed; c1900. **P.55:** "May loving angels . . . " from an entry in the autograph book of Viola Catherine Maurer, signed "With love, Mamma" and dated 1888. Scrap; 11½"h × 8½"w; die cut embossed; c 1890. Scraps; die cut, embossed; c1900. **P.56:** Foldout valentine; 8 stages, die cut, embossed, gilded, applied scrap, gold embossed trim, honeycomb tissue, printed gelatin film; Germany: inscribed 1910. Child's fan; ostrich feather; c1890. **P.57:** Foldout valentine (doors open as valentine folds down); 8 stages, die cut, embossed, gilded, applied scrap, silver glitter, honeycomb tissue, gelatin film; Germany; 1910; **P.58–59:** Boxed valentine novelty ("A daisy chain"); die cut, silk ribbon; Ernest Nister, London; printed in Bavaria; c1895. Foldout valentine; 3 panels; 7½"h × 20⅛"w; die cut, embossed, gilded, gold-stamped greeting;

c1910. **P.60:** Stock advertising calendar; full size, 17¼"h × 9½"w; die cut, embossed, gilded; imprinted Audubon Roller Mills, Audubon, Minn.; Germany; 1904. Fan; ostrich feather, faux tortoiseshell; c1890.

"FORGET NOT THY FRIEND"

P.61: Cotillion badge; embossed gold foil over paper, gathered mesh, gold and silver embossed ornaments, silk ribbon; c1875. Scraps; die cut, embossed; c1880. Hidden-name visiting cards: Embossed border, applied scrap; c1885. Die-cut edge, applied scrap; c1890. Die cut, applied scrap, gilded; c1885. Envelope; aplied scrap, die cut, embossed card inside; c1890. Die cut, applied scrap; c1895. Scrap; die cut, embossed; c1880. Hidden-name visiting cards: Die cut, tinted edges, applied scrap, gilded; c1895. Die cut, silver and tinted edge, applied scrap; c1890. **P.62:** Beads; faux mother-of-pearl; c1920. Postcard; embossed; Germany; c1910. Scrap; die cut, embossed; c1900. Postcards: S. Langsdorf, Germany; c1910. A.&M.B., Germany; c1900. S. Langsdorf, Germany; c1910. S. Langsdorf, Germany; postmarked 1908. Valentine (silk ribbon opens to reveal cloth swatch, needle, thread, button); paper lace; hand inscription; applied scrap, embossed gilded folder; c1865. Postcard; S. Langsdorf, Germany; postmarked 1909. Valentine; paper lace, applied scrap; c1865. Postcard; Helen Jackson, artist; Raphael Tuck, London; printed in Germany; c1905. **P.63:** Scrap; die cut, embossed; c1900. Valentine; embossed, applied silver foil scraps, hand coloring, Kershaw; c1860. Sachet; embossed, woven silk greeting applied from behind; c1860. Transformation paper novelty (door opens to reveal figure clothed); c1910. Postcards: Embossed; S. Langsdorf, Germany; c1910. Embossed; Souvenir Post Card Co., N.Y. and Berlin; c1910. Embossed; Germany; c1910. Embossed; Germany; c1910. **P.64:** "While the

bright sun . . . " calling-card verse. Shaped valentine; die cut, embossed, gilded; c1910. **P.65:** Stock advertising calendar; 12"h × 17½"w; die cut, embossed, gilded; imprinted Herman Damrow, Dry Goods Dealer, Firth Neb; 1910. Scrap figures; 11½"h; die cut, embossed; c1890. **P.66:** Scrap; die cut, embossed; c1880. Valentine; paper lace, gilded, applied scrap, paper springs; c1865. Valentine; gilded cameo lace; scrap applied from behind; inscribed 1865. Scrap; die cut, embossed; c1885. Valentine; chromolithographed cameo paper lace mounted on paper springs over embossed cover, applied scrap; c1865. Sachet folder; gilded paper lace, cameo paper lace mounted over cardboard covers, silk ribbon; c1860. Scrap; die cut, embossed; c1880. **P.67:** Scrap; die cut, embossed, gilded; c1885. Valentine (center lifts to reveal hidden message); paper lace, applied scrap; England; c1860. Religious valentine, S. Johanna; hand cutwork, hand-painted; c1750. Valentine folder; paper lace over cardboard covers, applied scrap, silk ribbon tie; c1870. Valentine; paper lace, paper motto, scrap applied from behind; c1860. Scrap; die cut, embossed; c1885. **P.68:** Fan; hand-painted silk, faux ivory; c1890. Stock

calendar illustration; die cut, embossed; tabs on top piece lock into slots for dimensional effect; c1905. **P.69:** "Loyal friendship . . . " calling-card verse. Scraps; die cut, embossed; c1885. **P.70:** "My Own Sweet Valentine" from *The Poetical Letter Writer*. Scrap; 10⅝"h × 8"w; die cut, embossed; c1890. **P.71:** Collage wreath of scraps; miniature scraps, hand-assembled; c1880. Scraps: die cut embossed; c1880–90. **P.72:** Pansy pins; enamel on gold, pearl, diamond; c1910. Foldout valentine; 6¼"h × 6¼"w; die cut, embossed; c1910. Scraps: die cut, embossed; c1885–95. **P.73:** Valentine; paper lace, chromolithographed center; E. Rimmel, London; c1865. Scraps: die cut, embossed; c1885. Miniature friendship card; embossed; c1885. Postcard; embossed; gilded padlock opens to reveal lady; John Winch; 1910. Scraps: die cut, embossed; c1880. **P.74:** Jacquard trim; silk; c1870. Shaped valentine; die cut, embossed, gilded, easel back; Germany; c1910. **P.75:** Foldout valentine; 2 stages, die cut, embossed, gilded, easel back; Germany; c1910. **P.76:** Drop valentine; die cut, embossed, silk ribbon; c1890. Valentine envelope; Ernest Nister, London; c1895. Scraps; die cut, embossed; c1880–90. Valentine; die cut; Raphael Tuck, London; printed in Saxony; c1905. Valentine envelope; embossed, applied scrap; Germany; inscribed 1914. Hidden-name card; applied scrap; c1885. Friendship card; embossed; inscribed 1903. Foldout valentine; 3 stages, die cut, embossed, Ernest Nister, London; printed in Bavaria; c1900. Hidden-name card; embossed, applied scrap, gilded; c1895. **P.77:** Foldout valentine; 4 stages, die cut, embossed; Germany; c1910. **P.78:** Postcard; embossed, silvered; Germany; c1910. **P.79:** Hold-to-light postcard; Germany; postmarked 1911. **P.80:** Mechanical friendship card (pull tab opens shutters to reveal lady, the whole mounted on heavy card); silk fringe, gold beveled edge, silk cord for hanging, tassels, brass caps; c1880.